FRENCH SHORT STORIES FOR BEGINNERS:

Become Fluent in Less Than 30 Days
Using a Proven Scientific Method
Applied in These Language Lessons.
Practice Vocabulary, Conversation & Grammar Daily
(series 2)

Table of Contents

INTRODUCTION

Welcome to "French Short Stories for Beginners: Become Fluent in Less Than 30 Days Using a Proven Scientific Method Applied in These 25 Lessons. Practice Vocabulary, Conversation and Grammar Daily (Part 1)". In this book, you will find a collection of short stories that will help you get a head start on learning French in a quick and simple fashion.

Learning French, like any other language, can be a challenging task. But it doesn't have to more challenging than it needs to. In fact, most books, methods and courses out there guarantee results in a short period of time. However, they don't take the time to present learners with the fundamentals that will enable them to make the most of their learning experience.

That is why this book is focused on providing you with the fundamentals that you will need in order to learn Spanish for the first time, or to brush up on your current skills. After all, why not make the most of your time and effort by learning another language?

As a matter of fact, being able to speak a foreign language, not to mention multiple languages, is a skill which is always in demand. While you may not actually get a job based on your linguistic competence alone, your ability to speak other languages will set you apart from anyone else in the business world.

What is you are keen on learning French because you would like to travel? Then we've got you covered, too. You can take these lessons as a means of getting a grasp on the fundamentals that you will need in order to navigate your way through French-speaking countries. If you are learning French because you are looking to take on a new challenge, then by all means, go right ahead and take advantage of this opportunity to do so.

The fact of the matter is that learning French doesn't have to an overwhelming task. With the tips, techniques and strategies that we will outline in this book, you will have a very good sense of how you can go about using the lessons contained herein to improve your French skills. Furthermore, you will be able to learn how to learn any language as the tips, techniques and strategies can be applied to virtually any language out there.

So, what are you waiting for?

The longer you wait to take on this challenge, the longer it will take you to achieve your goal of speaking another language. Whether French is your second language, or your third, fourth, fifth, and so on, you will find the content in this book easy to manage. As such, you won't have to work harder than you have to. You will have the right tools to achieve your goals in the shortest amount of time possible.

Please bear in mind that there is one essential ingredient in learning French, or any language for that matter: consistency. Please make the effort to be consistent in your endeavors to learn this wonderful language. You will find that consistency will make things a lot easier for you. See you on the inside.

Section *1*:
Fundamentals of Learning French

Chapter 1:
Tips and Strategies for Learning French

In this chapter, we will be taking a look at useful tips, techniques and strategies which you can use to learn French. As a matter of fact, the information contained in this chapter can be easily extrapolated to the learning of any language and not just French. As such, you can feel confident that the content in this chapter is applicable well beyond this book.

For most folks, learning a language can seem like a daunting task. The main reason behind this lies in the fact that most folks are unfamiliar with the dynamic of learning a language. Consequently, they don't really know where to begin and how to make the most of their efforts.

Hence, many language learners tend to quit after a while because they can't seem to gain enough traction. This leads to frustration as struggling with a new language is never a pleasant experience. However, much of the frustration and struggles can be avoided by learning the ropes of how languages work.

The underpinnings of any language lie in the way the language is structured. In the case of French, its basis lies in the conjugation of verbs. This means that you must become familiar with the various verb conjugations in order to fully understand how to structure the various verb tenses used throughout the language.

This can be a bit complicated with Romance languages. So Spanish, English, Italian, Portuguese and Romanian receive the denomination of "Romance" languages since they are mainly derived from Latin which was the language of the old Roman Empire.

Over the centuries, each one of these languages has acquired its own nuances that make it unique. While they all have the same underpinnings, the visible surface can be quite different. Thus, it is important to get a firm understanding of how these languages work.

In this book, we will predominantly focus on the present tense as it is the most widely used tense in the French language. Most French speakers tend to use what are known as "simple" tenses since they tend to focus on just one tense at a time.

This is a stark contrast to the English language as most English speakers are able to weave their way in and out of various verb tenses. This can make conversation rather complex especially when topics warrant the use of several verb tenses.

The starting point with the French language lies with the infinitive form of verbs. Verbs that do not have a verb tense are known as "infinitives". In other words, this is their pure form prior to being conjugated into a specific verb tense. In English, the infinitive form of verbs is written out as "to play" for example.

In French, the infinitive form of verbs is defined by the ending of each verb. As such, there are three main forms in which infinitive verbs end. This is what will become the basis of the conjugation for each verb.

The other factor that will determine the manner in which a verb must be conjugated is the subject of the sentence. This is exactly the same as English. As such, depending on the subject that agrees with the verb, the verb must be conjugated in a specific manner.

So, let's take a look at the subject pronouns which can be used in French.

- Je(I)
- Tu (you, singular)
- Il (he)
- Elle (she)
- Nous (we)
- Vous (you, plural)
- Ils (they, masculine)
- Elles (they, feminine)

This list above presents the subject pronouns which are used in the French language. Thus, this opens the door for a couple of important aspects to consider.

First of all, you will notice that there are singular and plural subject pronouns. So, "Tu es un enseignant" and "Vous êtes enseignants" use the singular and plural subject pronoun though its function is different.

Please note that English is an outlier in this regard as virtually all languages make a distinction between the singular and plural versions of "you". As such, it is important to keep this mind as you navigate throughout the texts and conversation you find in French.

Another important distinction between English and most other languages, especially Romance languages, is the use of the masculine and feminine for nouns. French is a gender language. What this means is that nouns do receive a "male" or "female" denomination.

French assigns a gender to all nouns. This might get a bit tricky as determining which nouns are masculine and which nouns are feminine can be tough. But rest assured that with practice and experience, you will be able to get a firm grasp on this. We will be taking a deeper look at this in the next chapter.

One other fundamental difference between Romance languages and French is the various ways in which you can address a person. In French, there are two main forms in which you can address a person. The most common form is "Tu". It can be used to address people of a similar age, station or friends, family and other acquaintances with whom you have a high degree of familiarity.

In the case of "Vous", this form is used to refer to people who are much older than you, have a higher station, such as an employer, or people with whom you are not very familiar, for example, new acquaintances whom you've just met.

With these fundamentals in mind, let's take a look at learning strategies which you can use throughout this book.

- Consistency is the biggest success factor you will encounter when learning a language. Regardless of whether you can devote 15 minutes, or 2 hours a day, the most important thing to keep in mind is that a consistent amount of time dedicated to learning will go a long way.

In this regard, most folks "binge learn", that is, they will not touch their books for days and then spend hours on end trying to make the time. Think about it along these lines: imagine you do not go to the gym for a week and then you decide to spend 3 hours working out on a Saturday morning. What do you think the result of that would be?

The same principle applies to language learning.

- Repetition is another success factor. When you go over your lessons multiple times, you will be able to better fixate information and knowledge into your mind. After all, humans are not built to learn things instantaneously. Humans need practice and repetition before they can master any skill. That same concept applies to language. The more practice you get, the more your skills will improve.

- Keep a learning diary. Keeping a learning diary, or a log of your activities, will help you visualize what you are doing to help yourself learn. In other words, you are keeping track of your language learning tasks. What this does is help you to see what works and doesn't. Later on, you can always refer back to those tasks which are providing you with the most value and which ones are not.

- Making handwritten notes will help fixate knowledge much better. Of course, using your phone, laptop or tablet makes life a lot easier. However, making handwritten notes enables the brain to involve more senses in the learning process. As such, individual words and grammar will permeate your mind in such a way that the mechanics of grammar, word order and spelling become clear in your mind.

- Use a tool such as www.linguee.fr as a grammar and conjugation reference. In addition, this tool will also provide you with the pronunciation of words. Consequently, you will have a tool that can support you when you are working on your own. Furthermore, it is a great study tool or just serve as a reference when you are curious about something related to your French lessons.

Now, let's look at a suggested methodology which you can use to help you get the most out of this book. Of course, this is not the only way that you can take advantage of the material in this book. Nevertheless, this methodology is designed to help you utilize the contents of this book to the fullest.

- Firstly, read each story once, all the way through. At first, it will be hard to make sense of its contents. However, as you go through the story, you will see some words which resemble English words. These words, most of the time, will basically be the same French words. So, you can highlight, or underline, these words and make note of them.

- Next, go through the text a second time. You will see your comprehension improving significantly. You will notice how similar-looking and sounding words make the text a lot easier to understand.

- After, go through the text highlighting, or underlining, words which are completely unfamiliar to you. Hopefully they won't be that many, but there will be some of these words. This will help you to visualize how much of the vocabulary is actually new to you.

- Then, you can use a tool such as www.linguee.fr or www.wordreference.com to help you find the meaning, pronunciation and usage of these new vocabulary items.

- Once you have found translations, synonyms and equivalent meanings, you can then proceed to run through the entire text one more time. You will find that the text is now much more comprehensible that it once was. This will enable you to make greater sense of the content in each lesson.
- After you feel comfortable with the language in the lesson, you can proceed to the questions located at the end of the lesson. The questions are intended to help you gain further practice into question formation, word order and reading comprehension. The questions have been designed to be open-ended. As such, there is no single way of answering. Nevertheless, we have taken care to provide suggested responses in order to provide you with guidance.
- Once you feel confident in answering each question, you go back and give the text one more run through. You can read the text aloud for further practice. If you are shy about your pronunciation, pick a time when you are alone and go through it.
- If you so choose, you can use a tool such as the Text to French plugin for Google Chrome to read the text for you. This will give you a great sense of how the text is pronounced. As such, you will be able to get the perfect pronunciation and thereby help you get the right pronunciation as well.
- One good tip is to have a vocabulary notebook. You can use your learning journal to write down all of the vocabulary words which you encounter on a daily basis. What this enables you to do is to keep track of all the new words that you learn on a given day. Thus, the act of writing things down by hand will help to further fixate ideas in your mind.
- Lastly, watching French language content on television or online will also help you to practice your listening skills while allowing you to learn more vocabulary and grammar. So, do try to make the most of the opportunities around to improve your French skills.

With these tips and strategies, you will be well on your way to improving your overall French skills. In the next chapter we will be taking a closer look at language aspects which tend to be particularly tricky for English speakers.

Chapter 2:
Common Problems when Learning French

In this chapter, we are going to be looking at the various problem areas that English speakers generally tend to have when they seek out to learn French. As such, we will be going over them in this chapter so as to provide insight and recommendations on how to deal with them as you progress through your French learning endeavors.

Earlier, we established that French, just like English and Italian, is a Romance language. In contrast, English is of Germanic origin. What this means is that English and French were born in different neighbourhood. The influence of French upon the English language has led it to have some striking similarities with French. However, there is enough difference between both languages to throw a monkey wrench into anyone's learning endeavours.

What does this mean?

It means that when English speakers go about learning French, they will run into some essential differences that will be challenging at first, but don't necessarily have to insurmountable. As such, it is important to understand these differences in order to make them more accessible to learners.

The first big difference is gender. The easiest way to identify gender among nouns is by observing the article that precedes it.

For example, "le, un" (the) is used for masculine and "la, une" (the) is used for feminine. So, "le soleil" (the sun) is masculine whereas "la lune" (the moon) is feminine. This is a good rule of thumb to follow when you are reading a text or simply hearing regular conversation.

However, it gets tricky when you see, or think, of an object but you are unaware of the article that precedes it. In this case, it can be tough to figure out the gender of an object. Since there really is no way to determine this just by looking at the object itself, there is one way in which you can figure this out: look at the object's name.

For instance, these are some examples of masculine nouns:

- La voiture (a car)
- Le garçon (a boy)
- Un baton (a stick)
- Le singe (a monkey)

As you can see, these nouns are all masculine given their articles. Also, there are some exceptions which you can keep an eye out for.

Here are some examples of feminine nouns:

- La chaussure (a shoe)
- Une maison (a house)
- La plante (a plant)
- La maman (a mother)
- Une feuille (a leaf)

Also, another good rule of thumb is that nouns can be converted into feminine. For instance, "infirmier" which is masculine, can become feminine as "infirmière".

Please keep in mind that French always uses the articles "le, un" and "la, une" to precede the reference to a noun. Conversely, English does not use this form unless the speaker is being specific about the noun in question.

With this guide, you can begin to navigate your way through the world of masculine and feminine nouns. As you gain more practice and experience, you will find that it is actually rather straightforward. So, do take the time to go over them.

Another area to take into consideration is verb conjugation.

Unlike English, French has a specific verb conjugation for verbs based on the subject that it agrees with and the verb tense.

This is rather simple and straightforward in the English language as verb conjugation does not necessarily imply radically modifying the verb's structure. However, French does require verb endings to be changed in accordance to the subject it agrees with. But fear not, we will make this very straightforward.

The first thing to look out for the ending of the verb in its infinitive form. As stated earlier, the infinitive form of a verb is when it has not been conjugated to agree with a subject in a particular verb tense. As such, the infinitive form of the verb is key in order to determine how it will be conjugated.

Verbs in the infinitive form in French will end in one of three ways: "er", "re" and "ir". So, let's take a look at some examples of this:

- Verbs ending in "er"
- Manger (to eat)
- Jouer (to play)
- Voyager (to travel)
- Chanter (to sing)
- Signer (to sign)

Now, let's take a look at some verbs that end in "re":

- Verbs ending in "re":
- Prendre (to take)
- Vivre (to live)
- Vendre (to sale)
- Résoudre (to solve)
- Rendre (to return)

Here is a list of some verbs ending in "ir":

- Verbs ending in "ir"
- Ouvrir (to open)
- Dormir (to sleep)
- Sentir (to feel)
- Venir (to come)
- Finir (to finish)

The above examples are a small sample size of the verbs which you will encounter throughout your study of the French language. As such, let's take a look at how these verbs are conjugated in the present simple tense.

Here is a chart which explains the various endings for each subject and according to the verb ending.

Pronom sujet	MANGER (To eat)	DORMIR (To sleep)	PRENDRE (To take)
Je	Mange	Dors	prends
Tu	Manges	Dors	prends
Il/Elle	Mange	Dort	prend
Nous	mangeons	dormons	prenons
Vous	Mangez	dormez	prenez
Ils/Elles	mangent	dorment	prennent

Figure 1: Verb endings in the present simple tense.

The charts above show the endings that are to be attached depending on the subject that a verb will agree with. Hence, let's take a look at some examples in order to make this point evident.

- Infinitive: chanter (to sing)
- Je chante (I sing)
- Tu chantes (you sing, singular)
- Il chante (he sings)
- Elle chante (she sings)
- Nous chantons (we sing)
- Vous chantez (you sing, plural)
- Ils chantent (they sing, masculine)
- Elles chantent (they sing, feminine)

As you can see, the original "er" ending is dropped in favour of the corresponding ending based on the subject. With the exception of a handful of irregular verbs, this is the rule of thumb to follow with verbs ending in "er".

Consequently, the same pattern applies to the verbs ending in "re" and "ir". Let's have a look at some examples.

- Infinitive: Vivre (To live)
- Je vis (I live)
- Tu vis (you live, singular)
- Il vit (he lives)
- Elle vit (she lives)
- Nous vivons (we live)
- Vous vivez (you live, plural)
- Ils vivent (they live, masculine)
- Elles vivent (they live, feminine)

As with the "re" verbs, the "ir" ending is dropped in favour of the corresponding ending. Let's take a look at an example of an "ir" verb.

- Infinitive: Courir (to run)
- Je cours (I run)
- Tu cours (you run, singular)
- Il court (he runs)
- Elle court (she runs)
- Nous courons (we run)
- Vous courez (you run, plural)
- Ils courent (they run, masculine)
- Elles courent (they run, feminine)

Given the previous examples, the conjugation of verbs in the present simple are rather straightforward. Of course, it takes some time and practice. Nevertheless, you can become proficient with verb conjugations in a relatively short period of time. As such, all you need is to dedicate some time and effort in to practicing the way verbs are to be conjugated. If you are ever in doubt, www.linguee.fr is a great tool which you can consult in order to get the right conjugation.

On other significant difference between English and French is the use of subjects, or lack thereof, in sentences. In French it is quite common to omit the use of a subject at the beginning of sentence especially when it is clear who is being referred to in the conversation. As such, speakers will often take the liberty of omitting the subject observing only the proper conjugation of the verb.

Needless to say, this can cause confusion even among native French speakers. The reason for this is that unless there is a clear understanding of who is being referred to, it can be very difficult to keep track of a conversation.

Let's look at an example:

- Je viens des Etats-Unis (I am from the United States).

In this example, the use of the from "je viens" (I am from) is the proper conjugation for the verb "venir" (to come) in the present simple tense. However, a French speaker would be more aware to the fact that it is perfectly clear that this individual is referring to themselves.

So, do keep an eye out for this type of expression as you will frequently see it throughout the text presented in this book.

On the subject of the auxiliary verbs, the French language has two versions of the auxiliary verbs: "être" (to be) and "avoir" (to have). As such, let's take a look at their difference and their conjugation. In essence, "Avoir" is generally used to show that the subject owns/ has something or someone, example: La petite fille a mangé du gâteau (The little girl ate cake.) and "Être" is generally used to express a condition or attitude of the subject concerned, example:Je suis professeur de français (I am a French teacher). This makes it clear that your occupation is permanent and won't be changing any time soon. On the other hand, you can say "Je suis heureux" (I am happy). This is a totally changeable proposition as your mood is far more changeable that your occupation.

The distinction with "être" (to be) in French are very useful when you are talking about yourself, or perhaps you are talking about the way you feel and the location of people and things. Consequently, the conjugation of each verb is also different.

Let's look at the conjugation of those verbs:

ÊTRE	AVOIR
Je suis malade.	J'ai une belle maison.
Tu es heureuse	Tu as un vieux cartable.
Il/Elle est malade.	Il/Elle a trois voitures.
Nous sommes en vacance.	Nous avons du travail.
Vous êtes en retard.	Vous avez du temps.
Ces enfants sont très aimables	Ils/Elles ont un téléphone

Now, the present continuous (le gérondif) is used in exactly the same fashion as it is in English; the present continuous is used to indicate when there is a temporary action either happening at the time of speaking or around the time of speaking. Thus, the most important element to consider is that the present continuous is a temporary action whereas the present simple (l'indicatif présent) is used to indicate more permanent actions.

The present continuous (le gérondif) is a verbal form. In French, it is formed as a present participle proceeded by the preposition "en" (in), and is one of the seven modes of grammar. Its subject being always the same as that of the conjugated verb, the present continuous (le gérondif) can never be the center of a proposition..

Here are some examples:

- Il marche en boitant (He walks in limp).
- En mangeant moins, vous vous porteriez mieux (By eating less, you'd be better off).
- Je l'ai aperçu en arrivant (I saw it on my way in).

Please notice that this ending is not specific to the subject. Therefore, the main verb does need to be transformed to suit the individual subject in question. This makes it far easier to get a grasp on this tense as you won't have to conjugate each verb based on individual subjects.

With this, we have laid the groundwork for the content in this book. We are now ready to move on to the short stories prepared for your study. Please keep in mind that nothing is ever cast in stone when it comes to language. Nevertheless, the patterns which we have laid out herein will provide you with a good head start when it comes to improving your French skills.

The main thing to keep in mind is that consistency will give you the best chance to improve your skills regardless of your starting point. Hence, if you can devote a certain amount of time, on a regular basis, the likelihood of your French skills improving will increase significantly.

So, please sit back and enjoy the short stories that have been prepared for you. They are designed to be both educational and entertaining. Please remember to go over them as many times as you need so that you can get the most out of the contents and materials presented in this book.

Let's move on to the next section in this book.

Section 2:
The Verb "Être"

Lesson 1:
Present Simple with verb "être"

English On vacation	En vacance
Important vocabulary: welcome shows stars frequented must-see impressive full majestic landscapes recognized	**Vocabulaire important:** bienvenue spectacles stars fréquenté voir absolument impressionnant entières majestueux paysages reconnus
The United States is a very big country. But it is also a very beautiful and exciting country. The **landscapes** are impressive from coast to coast. The north is cold. The south is warm. The beaches are beautiful and relaxing. The mountains are large and **majestic**.	Les États-Unis sont un très grand pays. Mais c'est aussi un pays très beau et passionnant. Les **paysages** sont impressionnants d'un océan à l'autre. Le nord est froid. Le sud est chaud. Les plages sont magnifiques et relaxantes. Les montagnes sont grandes et **majestueuses**.
The most famous cities in the United States are New York, Miami, Chicago and Washington, DC. These cities are famous for their famous sites and **shows**. Broadway is well known in New York. Also, its Central Park and the Statue of Liberty are tourist attractions **frequented** by visitors.	Les villes les plus célèbres des États-Unis sont New York, Miami, Chicago et Washington, DC. Ces villes sont célèbres pour leurs sites et **spectacles** célèbres. Broadway est bien connu à New York. De plus, son parc central et la statue de la Liberté sont des attractions touristiques **fréquentées** par les visiteurs.
The beach in Miami is known all over the world. Miami Beach is frequented by **stars** and famous people. Life is calm and relaxed in Miami. The people are kind and calm. It is a city to go on vacation. In Chicago, the Sears Tower is well known. Museums, theaters and restaurants are also **recognized** in Chicago. In short, Chicago is a very exciting city. It is a city to visit with friends and family. Washington DC is an **impressive** city. In Washington, the monuments are recognized all over the world. If you are a lover of art and culture, Washington is the perfect city. All the historical sites in Washington are wonderful. My favorite	La plage de Miami est connue dans le monde entier. Miami Beach est fréquentée par des **stars** et des gens célèbres. La vie est calme et détendue à Miami. Les gens sont gentils et calmes. C'est une ville pour des vacances. À Chicago, la Sears Tower est bien connue. Les musées, théâtres et restaurants sont également **reconnus** à Chicago. Bref, Chicago est une ville très excitante. C'est une ville à visiter entre amis et en famille. Washington DC est une ville **impressionnante**. À Washington, les monuments sont reconnus dans le monde entier. Si vous aimez l'art et la culture,

place is the monument is the monument to Abraham Lincoln. The White House is also a **must-see** place. It's a pleasure to visit Washington.	Washington est la ville parfaite. Tous les sites historiques de Washington sont merveilleux. Mon endroit préféré est le monument dédié à Abraham Lincoln. La Maison-Blanche est aussi un lieu **incontournable**. C'est un plaisir de visiter Washington.
My favorite city in the United States is San Antonio, Texas. My favorite place is The Alamo. It is such a special monument and **full** of history. All of you, my friends, are **welcome** to San Antonio. San Antonio is a city for all tastes. The restaurants are wonderful. The tourist attractions are unique. The theaters and museums are interesting. The sports teams are the best. San Antonio is the best place to vacation.	Ma ville préférée aux États-Unis est San Antonio, Texas. Mon endroit préféré est l'Alamo. C'est un monument si spécial et **plein** d'histoire. Vous tous, mes amis, êtes les **bienvenus** à San Antonio. San Antonio est une ville pour tous les goûts. Les restaurants sont merveilleux. Les attractions touristiques sont uniques. Les théâtres et les musées sont intéressants. Les équipes sportives sont les meilleures. San Antonio est le meilleur endroit pour les vacances.
Please answer the following questions.	Veuillez répondre aux questions suivantes.
What are the United States like?	Comment sont les États-Unis?
What are the landscapes like?	Comment sont les paysages?
What are the most famous cities in the United States?	Quelles sont les villes les plus célèbres des États-Unis?
What are the famous sites in New York?	Quels sont les sites célèbres de New York?
Who frequents the beach in Miami?	Qui fréquente la plage de Miami?

_____	_____
What are the people like in Miami?	Comment sont les gens à Miami?
What is Chicago like?	Comment est Chicago?
What is my favorite monument?	Quel est mon monument préféré?
What is my favorite city?	Quelle est ma ville préférée?
What is the best place to go on vacation?	Quel est le meilleur endroit pour partir en vacances?

Suggested answers	Réponses suggérées
What are the United States like? The United States is a large, beautiful and exciting country.	Comment sont les États-Unis? Les États-Unis sont un pays vaste, beau et passionnant.
What are the landscapes like? The landscapes are impressive from coast to coast.	Comment sont les paysages? Les paysages sont impressionnants d'un océan à l'autre.
What are the most famous cities in the United States? The most famous cities in the United States are: New York, Chicago, Miami and Washington DC.	Quelles sont les villes les plus célèbres des États-Unis? Les villes les plus célèbres des États-Unis sont: New York, Chicago, Miami et Washington DC.
What are the famous sites in New York? The Statue of Liberty, Central Park and Broadway are the most famous sites in New York	Quels sont les sites célèbres de New York? La Statue de la Liberté, Central Park et Broadway sont les sites les plus célèbres de New York.
Who frequents the beach in Miami? Stars and famous people frequent the beach in Miami.	Qui fréquente la plage de Miami? Des stars et des gens célèbres fréquentent la plage de Miami.
What are the people like in Miami? The people are kind and calm.	Comment sont les gens à Miami? Les gens sont gentils et calmes.
What is Chicago like? Chicago is an exciting and recognized city.	Comment est Chicago? Chicago est une ville passionnante et reconnue.
What is my favorite monument? The monument to Abraham Lincoln is my favorite.	Quel est mon monument préféré? Le monument à Abraham Lincoln est mon préféré.
What is my favorite city? San Antonio, Texas is my favorite city.	Quelle est ma ville préférée? San Antonio, Texas est ma ville préférée.
What is the best place to go on vacation? San Antonio, Texas is the best place to vacation.	Quel est le meilleur endroit pour partir en vacances? San Antonio, Texas est le meilleur endroit pour les vacances.

Lesson 2:
Present Simple with verb "être"

English My House	Mon Domicile
Important vocabulary: spacious old appliances drawers comfortable huge functional rooms half backyard perhaps	**Vocabulaire important:** spacieux de longue date électroménager caleçon confortables colossal fonctionnel pièces demi arrière-cour peut-être
My house is the most beautiful place in the whole world. It is not very big, but it is very **comfortable**. It is an **old** house. It is considered part of the history of my community. It is also part of my family's history. My family and I are happy in this house.	Ma maison est le plus bel endroit du monde. Il n'est pas très grand, mais il est très **confortable**. C'est une **vieille** maison. C'est considéré comme faisant partie de l'histoire de ma communauté. Cela fait aussi partie de l'histoire de ma famille. Ma famille et moi sommes heureux dans cette maison.
The **rooms** in my house are not big, but they are very comfortable. There are four in total. My room's color is nice. The furniture is **functional** with lots of space. The television in my room is big. The movies are incredible on this television.	Les **pièces** de ma maison ne sont pas grandes, mais elles sont très confortables. Il y en a quatre au total. La couleur de ma chambre est chouette. Le mobilier est **fonctionnel** avec beaucoup d'espace. La télévision dans ma chambre est grande. Les films sont incroyables sur cette télévision.
The bathrooms are **spacious** and well decorated. There are two bathrooms on the second level and one on the first level. In fact, the bathroom on the first level is **half** a bathroom. But it is very comfortable for the visitors to our house. My bathroom is perfect for me. It's all I need.	Les salles de bains sont **spacieuses** et bien décorées. Il y a deux salles de bains au deuxième niveau et une au premier niveau. En fait, la salle de bains du premier étage est la **moitié** d'une salle de bains. Mais il est très confortable pour les visiteurs de notre maison. Ma salle de bain est parfaite pour moi. C'est tout ce dont j'ai besoin.
The kitchen is big. The **appliances** are modern and useful. The refrigerator is very broad. The stove is easy to use. All utensils are stored in the kitchen **drawers**.	La cuisine est grande. Les **appareils** sont modernes et utiles. Le réfrigérateur est très large. La cuisinière est facile à utiliser. Tous les ustensiles sont rangés dans les **tiroirs** de la cuisine.
The family room is my favorite place in my house. My brothers and I are happy here. Television is **huge**. Basketball games are awesome on this television. We are not fans	La salle familiale est mon endroit préféré dans

of the same team, but of the sport. My father is a lover of cinema and my mother of telenovelas. The television is ideal for the whole family.

Perhaps the most impressive place in my house is the **backyard**. It is the ideal space for our dog, Max. Max is happy with all this space. We are a united family. That is why this house is the ideal size for us. Big houses are very nice, but we are happy with our small house. It is the best for our family.

ma maison. Mes frères et moi sommes heureux ici. La télévision est **énorme**. Les matchs de basket sont géniaux sur cette télévision. Nous ne sommes pas fans de la même équipe, mais du sport. Mon père est un amoureux du cinéma et ma mère de télénovelas. La télévision est idéale pour toute la famille.

L'endroit le plus impressionnant de ma maison est peut-être la **cour arrière**. C'est l'endroit idéal pour notre chien, Max. Max est content de tout cet espace. Nous sommes une famille unie. C'est pourquoi cette maison est la taille idéale pour nous. Les grandes maisons sont très jolies, mais nous sommes satisfaits de notre petite maison. C'est le meilleur pour notre famille.

Please answer the following questions.	Veuillez répondre aux questions suivantes.
What is my house like?	Comment est ma maison?
How is my house considered?	Comment ma maison est-elle considérée?
What are the rooms in my house like?	Comment sont les pièces de ma maison?
What is the furniture like?	Comment sont les meubles?
Where are the bathrooms?	Où sont les toilettes?
What is my bathroom like?	Comment est ma salle de bains?
What is my favorite place?	Quel est mon endroit préféré?
What is the most impressive place in the	Quel est l'endroit le plus impressionnant

house?	de la maison?
_____	_____
_____	_____
_____	_____
_____	_____
Who is Max?	**Qui est Max?**
_____	_____
_____	_____
_____	_____
_____	_____
What are big houses like?	**Comment sont les grandes maisons?**
_____	_____
_____	_____
_____	_____
_____	_____

Suggested answers	Réponses suggérées
What is my house like? My house is the most beautiful place in the world.	Comment est ma maison? Ma maison est le plus bel endroit du monde.
How is my house considered? My house is considered a part of my community's and my family's history.	Comment ma maison est-elle considérée? Ma maison fait partie de l'histoire de ma communauté et de ma famille.
What are the rooms in my house like? The rooms in my house are not very big, but they are very comfortable.	Comment sont les pièces de ma maison? Les pièces de ma maison ne sont pas très grandes, mais elles sont très confortables.
What is the furniture like? The furniture is functional and spacious.	Comment sont les meubles? Le mobilier est fonctionnel et spacieux.
Where are the bathrooms? There are two bathrooms on the second floor and one of the first floor.	Où sont les toilettes? Il y a deux salles de bains au deuxième étage et une du premier étage.
What is my bathroom like? My bathroom is perfecto for me. It's everything I need.	Comment est ma salle de bains? Ma salle de bain est parfaite pour moi. C'est tout ce dont j'ai besoin.
What is my favorite place? The family room is my favorite place.	Quel est mon endroit préféré? La salle familiale est mon endroit préféré.
What is the most impressive place in the house? Perhaps the backyard is the most impressive place in my house.	Quel est l'endroit le plus impressionnant de la maison? L'arrière-cour est peut-être l'endroit le plus impressionnant de ma maison.
Who is Max? Max is our dog.	Qui est Max? Max est notre chien.
What are big houses like? Big houses are nice.	Comment sont les grandes maisons? Les grandes maisons sont bien.

Lesson 3:
Present Simple with verb "être"

English The Kids at School	Les enfants à l'école
Important vocabulary: previous silent tired dynamic entertained restless game language teacher nagging puzzle	**Vocabulaire important:** antérieures muet fatigué dynamique diverti agité gibier langage instituteur hystérique énigme

Today, the children are happy at school. Their **teacher** is not in the class. A new teacher is with them. The regular teacher is very angry and **nagging**. This new teacher is very affectionate. She is kind to all the children. The children are happy with the new teacher.
 	
The previous teacher is very strict. The teacher is always serious. She is a good teacher and her students are good students, but the children are always quiet. The teacher is happy when the children are with their exercises in math, **language**, science.
 	
The new teacher is a young girl. She is **dynamic** and creative. The children are enthusiastic about their jobs and tasks.
 	
    •   "We are happy!"
 	
Yes, today the children are happy.
 	
    •   "I am very happy with you, too!"
 	
The kids in this class are very **restless**.
 	
    •   "Are you tired of playing?"
The new teacher is in a **game** with her kids.
    •   "We are not tired!"
 	
The kids are not tired of the games; games games and more games.
	Aujourd'hui, les enfants sont heureux à l'école. Leur **professeur** n'est pas en classe. Un nouveau professeur est avec eux. Le professeur habituel est très en colère et très **agacé**. Ce nouveau professeur est très affectueux. Elle est gentille avec tous les enfants. Les enfants sont satisfaits du nouvel enseignant.
	
	L'ancien professeur est très strict. Le professeur est toujours sérieux. C'est une bonne enseignante et ses élèves sont de bons élèves, mais les enfants sont toujours calmes. L'enseignant est heureux quand les enfants sont avec leurs exercices de mathématiques, de **langues**, de sciences.
	
	Le nouveau professeur est une jeune fille. Elle est **dynamique** et créative. Les enfants sont enthousiasmés par leur travail et leurs devoirs.
	    • "Nous sommes heureux!"
	
	Oui, aujourd'hui les enfants sont heureux.
	    • "Moi aussi, je suis très heureuse avec toi!"
	
	Les enfants de cette classe sont très **agités**.
	    • "T'en as marre de jouer?"
	La nouvelle prof **joue** avec ses enfants.
	    • "Nous ne sommes pas fatigués!"
	
	Les enfants ne sont pas fatigués des jeux; des jeux et encore des jeux.

The children's favorite game is "memory." Some children are **entertained** with this game. Other children are busy with a very large **puzzle**. The teacher is sure that these games are educational for her kids.

- "It is mealtime."

The kids are in their places with their food
- "Healthy food is important for growth. They are healthy thanks to the good food. "

The kids are silent for just a moment. The food is very good. Apples, oranges and bananas are the children's favorite snacks. Now they are satisfied.

- "It's time play!"

The children are ready for more games. Now they are not **silent**. They are ready for fun with their new teacher. But it's only for today. Their regular teacher is ready for tomorrow.

Le jeu préféré des enfants est "memory". Certains enfants sont **divertis** avec ce jeu. D'autres enfants sont occupés avec un très grand **puzzle**. L'enseignante est certaine que ces jeux sont éducatifs pour ses enfants.

- "C'est l'heure du repas."

Les enfants sont à leur place avec leur nourriture.
- "Une alimentation saine est importante pour la croissance. Ils sont en bonne santé grâce à la bonne nourriture."

Les enfants se taisent un instant. La nourriture est très bonne. Les pommes, les oranges et les bananes sont les collations préférées des enfants. Maintenant, ils sont satisfaits.

- "C'est l'heure de jouer!"

Les enfants sont prêts pour d'autres jeux. Maintenant, ils ne sont plus **silencieux**. Ils sont prêts à s'amuser avec leur nouveau professeur. Mais c'est seulement pour aujourd'hui. Leur professeur habituel est prêt pour demain.

Please answer the following questions.	Veuillez répondre aux questions suivantes.
Why are the children happy at school today?	Pourquoi les enfants sont-ils heureux à l'école aujourd'hui?
What is the regular teacher like?	Comment est l'enseignant régulier?
When is the regular teacher happy?	Quand le professeur habituel est-il heureux?

What is the new teacher like?	Comment est le nouveau professeur?
_____ _____ _____ _____	_____ _____ _____ _____
What are the kids in this class like?	Comment sont les enfants dans cette classe?
_____ _____ _____ _____	_____ _____ _____
What is the children's favorite game?	Quel est le jeu préféré des enfants?
_____ _____ _____ _____	_____ _____ _____
What are the children's games?	Quels sont les jeux des enfants?
_____ _____ _____	_____ _____ _____
What is the children's food?	Qu'est-ce que les enfants mangent?
_____ _____ _____	_____ _____ _____
What time is it?	Quelle heure est-il?
_____ _____ _____ _____	_____ _____ _____
When is the regular teacher ready?	Quand le professeur habituel sera-t-il prêt?
_____ _____ _____ _____	_____ _____ _____
Suggested answers	Réponses suggérées

Why are the children happy at school today? The regular teacher is not in class.	Pourquoi les enfants sont-ils heureux à l'école aujourd'hui? L'enseignant régulier n'est pas en classe.
What is the regular teacher like? The teacher is good, but she is strict, angry and nagging.	Comment est l'enseignant régulier? L'institutrice est bonne, mais elle est stricte, en colère et agaçante.
When is the regular teacher happy? She is happy when the kids are silent and with their exercises.	Quand le professeur habituel est-il heureux? Il est heureux quand les enfants sont silencieux et avec leurs exercices.
What is the new teacher like? The new teacher is young, dynamic and creative.	Comment est le nouveau professeur? Le nouvel enseignant est jeune, dynamique et créatif.
What are the kids in this class like? The kids in this class are restless.	Comment sont les enfants dans cette classe? Les enfants de cette classe sont agités.
What is the children's favorite game? Memory is the children's favorite game.	Quel est le jeu préféré des enfants? La mémoire est le jeu préféré des enfants.
What are the children's games? The children's games are educational.	Quels sont les jeux des enfants? Les jeux des enfants sont éducatifs.
What is the children's food? Oranges, bananas and apples is the children's food.	Qu'est-ce que les enfants mangent? Les oranges, les bananes et les pommes sont la nourriture des enfants.
What time is it? It's time to play.	Quelle heure est-il? C'est l'heure de jouer.
When is the regular teacher ready? The regular teacher is ready for tomorrow.	Quand le professeur habituel sera-t-il prêt? Le professeur habituel est prêt pour demain.

Section *3:*
The Present Simple Tense

Lesson 4:
Present Simple with "ER" verbs

| English
A Teacher's Job | French
Le Métier d'Enseignant |
|---|---|
| **Important vocabulary:**
in addition
grades
anyone
teach
outside
skills
schedule
teenagers
reasons
useful | **Vocabulaire Important:**
de plus
échelons
personne
enseigner
à l'extérieur
qualifications
échéancier
adolescentes
motifs
utile |
Many people think that the work of a teacher is not difficult. Many people think that teachers only drink coffee all day. Others think that the work of the teachers is not demanding. But teachers work just like everyone else. These are some **reasons** why teachers work a lot.	Beaucoup de gens pensent que faire le travail d'enseignant n'est pas difficile. Beaucoup de gens pensent que les enseignants ne boivent du café que toute la journée. D'autres pensent que le travail des enseignants n'est pas exigeant. Mais les professeurs travaillent comme tout le monde. Voilà quelques-unes des **raisons** pour lesquelles les enseignants travaillent beaucoup.
First, teachers **teach** children, **teenagers** and adults. A good teacher works with everyone who wants to study. It does not matter who it is. A teacher is always ready to help **anyone** to study.	Tout d'abord, les enseignants **dispensentdes cours** aux enfants, aux **adolescents** et aux adultes. Un bon professeur travaille avec tous ceux qui veulent étudier. Peu importe qui c'est. Un professeur est toujours prêt à aider **n'importe qui** à étudier.
Second, a teacher's work **schedule** is not eight hours. Teachers always work **outside** of class. They always take work to class. A teacher always **grades** exams during the weekend or at night. **In addition**, every teacher reviews the work of their students in their free time. Many times, this extra work is not paid.	Deuxièmement, **l'horaire** de travail d'un enseignant n'est pas de huit heures. Les enseignants travaillent toujours **à l'extérieur** de la classe. Ils apportent toujours le travail en classe. Un professeur **note** toujours les examens pendant le week-end ou la nuit. **De plus**, chaque enseignant passe en revue le travail de ses élèves pendant leur temps libre. Souvent, ce travail supplémentaire n'est pas rémunéré.
Third, extracurricular activities take place in schools. Some students practice sports	

or artistic **skills**. Some teachers organize social activities or reinforcement classes. Some teachers train students for sports or academic competitions. Other teachers prepare their students for standardized tests.

With these examples, it is seen that the work of one teacher is equal to all the others. Sure, it's a different job from a lawyer, accountant or engineer. But it is not an easy job. To be a teacher you need discipline and a desire to help others. Thanks to the teachers, we are **useful** people to our community.

If you want to be a teacher, you need patience, dedication and dedication to service. With study and effort, you manage to be a good teacher. When you are a teacher you help your community to be a better place. We all appreciate the work of a good teacher in our community.

Troisièmement, des activités parascolaires ont lieu dans les écoles. Certains élèves pratiquent des sports ou des **activités** artistiques. Certains enseignants organisent des activités sociales ou des cours de renforcement. Certains enseignants forment des élèves pour des compétitions sportives ou académiques. D'autres enseignants préparent leurs élèves à des tests harmonisés.

Avec ces exemples, on voit que le travail d'un enseignant est égal à celui de tous les autres. Bien sûr, c'est un travail différent de celui d'un avocat, d'un comptable ou d'un ingénieur. Mais ce n'est pas une tâche facile. Pour être enseignant, il faut de la discipline et le désir d'aider les autres. Grâce aux enseignants, nous sommes des personnes **utiles** à notre communauté.

Si vous voulez devenir enseignant, vous avez besoin de patience, de dévouement et de loyauté au service. Avec de l'étude et de l'effort, vous réussissez à être un bon professeur. Quand vous êtes enseignant, vous aidez votre communauté à devenir un meilleur endroit. Nous apprécions tous le travail d'un bon enseignant dans notre communauté.

Please answer the following questions.	Veuillez répondre aux questions suivantes.
What do people think of a teacher's job? _____ _____ _____ _____	Que pensent les gens du métier d'enseignant? _____ _____ _____
Who do teachers teach? _____ _____ _____ _____	Qui sont les enseignants? _____ _____ _____
Who does a good teacher work with? _____ _____ _____ _____	Avec qui un bon professeur travaille-t-il? _____ _____ _____
What is a teacher's schedule? _____ _____ _____ _____	Quel est l'horaire d'un enseignant? _____ _____ _____
What do teachers grade? _____ _____ _____ _____	Quelle est la note des enseignants? _____ _____ _____
How is a teacher's job seen? _____ _____ _____ _____	Comment voit-on le travail d'un enseignant? _____ _____ _____
What does it take be a good teacher? _____ _____ _____ _____	Que faut-il pour être un bon professeur? _____ _____ _____

What do you need to be a good teacher? _____ _____ _____ _____	De quoi avez-vous besoin pour être un bon professeur? _____ _____ _____ _____
How can you become a good teacher? _____ _____ _____ _____	Comment devenir un bon professeur? _____ _____ _____ _____
Who appreciates the work of a teacher? _____ _____ _____ _____	Qui apprécie le travail d'un enseignant? _____ _____ _____ _____

Suggested answers	Réponses suggérées
What do people think of a teacher's job?	Que pensent les gens du métier d'enseignant?
People think that teachers only drink coffee.	Les gens pensent que les enseignants ne boivent que du café.
Who do teachers teach?	Qui sont les enseignants?
Teachers teach children, teenagers, and adults.	Les enseignants enseignent aux enfants, aux adolescents et aux adultes.
Who does a good teacher work with?	Avec qui un bon professeur travaille-t-il?
A good teacher works with anyone who wants to learn.	Un bon enseignant travaille avec tous ceux qui veulent apprendre.
What is a teacher's schedule?	Quel est l'horaire d'un enseignant?
A teacher's schedule is not eight hours. Teachers work outside of class.	L'emploi du temps d'un professeur n'est pas de huit heures. Les enseignants travaillent à l'extérieur de la classe.
What do teachers grade?	Quelle est la note des enseignants?
Teachers grade exams.	Examens de niveau des enseignants.
How is a teacher's job seen?	Comment voit-on le travail d'un enseignant?
A teacher's good is seen like any other job.	Le bien d'un professeur est vu comme n'importe quel autre travail.
What does it take be a good teacher?	Que faut-il pour être un bon professeur?
Patience, dedication and vocation are needed.	Patience, dévouement et vocation sont nécessaires.
What do you need to be a good teacher?	De quoi avez-vous besoin pour être un bon professeur?
Study and effort are needed if you want to become a good teacher.	L'étude et l'effort sont nécessaires si vous voulez devenir un bon professeur.
How can you become a good teacher?	Comment devenir un bon professeur?
You can become a good teacher when you support your community.	Vous pouvez devenir un bon enseignant lorsque vous soutenez votre communauté.
Who appreciates the work of a teacher?	Qui apprécie le travail d'un enseignant?
We all appreciate the work of a good teacher.	Nous apprécions tous le travail d'un bon professeur.

Lesson 5:
Present Simple with "ER" verbs

English At a Restaurant	French Au Restaurant
Important vocabulary:	**Vocabulaire Important:**
	Le beefsteak
beefsteak	Le menu
menu	La réponse
answer	difficile
difficult	ainsi
so	appeler
call	Le serveur
waiter	La commande
order	penser
think	demander
ask	heures de repas
mealtimes	

To **order** in a restaurant you only need some important phrases. It is not **difficult**, but you do need to practice some basic phrases to order your favorite foods.

Pour **commander** dans un restaurant, vous avez juste besoin de quelques phrases importantes. Ce n'est pas **difficile**, mais vous devez vous familiariser avec quelques phrases de base pour commander vos aliments préférés.

To start, there are three **mealtimes** per day: breakfast, lunch and dinner. But these mealtimes are also verbs. **So**, you *breakfast* in the morning, *lunch* in the afternoon and *dinner* at night. These are the verbs used to express the three times of food.

Tout d'abord, il y a trois **heures de repas** par jour : petit déjeuner, déjeuner et dîner. Mais ces heures de repas sont aussi des verbes. **Ainsi**, vous prenez le *petit déjeuner* le matin, le *déjeuner* dans l'après-midi et le *dîner* le soir. Ce sont les verbes utilisés pour exprimer les trois temps de repas.

Then, you need to talk to the waiter.

Ensuite, vous devez parler au serveur.

Ask the **waiter**:
* The **menu** please.

Demandez au **serveur**:
* Le **menu**, s'il vous plaît.

At this request, the waiter gives you the menu. After a few minutes, the waiter asks:
* Do you wish to order?

À cette demande, le serveur vous donne le menu. Quelques minutes après, le serveur vous demande :
- Souhaitez-vous commander ?

To this question you reply:
* I need another minute please. This gets you more time to **think** about your order. Then, tell the waiter:

À cette question, vous répondez :
- Donnez-moi une minute, s'il vous plaît. Cela vous donne plus de temps pour **réfléchir** à votre commande. Ensuite, dites au serveur :

* I wish to order

- Je souhaite commander

The waiter asks you:

Le serveur vous demande :

* What do you wish to order?

- Que souhaitez-vous commander?

You can **answer**:
* I wish to order _____.

Vous pouvez **répondre** :
- Je souhaite commander _____.

Your answer is about anything in the menu. An example is:

Votre réponse concerne tout ce qui se trouve dans le menu. Par exemple :
- Je voudrais commander un **beefsteak** avec des légumes et du riz.

* I wish to order a **beefsteak** with vegetables and rice.

Une autre possibilité est :
- Je souhaite commander du poulet grillé avec une salade.

Another possibility is:

- I wish to order grilled chicken with a salad.

Listen well when the waiter **asks**:

- What do you wish to drink?

Now, you must order your drink. Your answer is:

- I wish to drink _____.

You indicate your favorite drink to the waiter. The most popular drinks sodas, natural juices, mineral water, coffee or tea. An example is:

- I wish to drink sparkling mineral water.

After ordering, the waiter takes your drink while your food is prepared and cooked. Preparing food takes time. But your food is ready soon.

To pay for your food, **call** the waiter. Use this phrase:

- The bill please.

Shortly, the waiter takes the bill for your consumption. Pay and you go. Bon Appetit!

Écoutez bien quand le serveur vous **demande** :
- Que désirez-vous boire ?

Maintenant, vous devez commander votre boisson. Votre réponse est:
- Je désire boire _____.

Vous indiquez votre boisson préférée au serveur. Les boissons les plus populaires sont les sodas, les jus naturels, l'eau minérale, le café ou le thé.
Par exemple:
- Je souhaite boire de l'eau minérale gazeuse.

Après la commande, le serveur prend votre boisson pendant que votre plat est préparé et cuit. La préparation des aliments prend du temps. Mais votre repas est bientôt prêt.

Pour payer votre repas, **appelez** le serveur. Utilisez cette expression:
- L'addition, s'il vous plaît.

En peu de temps, le serveur prend la facture de votre consommation. Vous payez et vous partez. Bon Appétit!

Please answer the following questions.	Veuillez répondre aux questions suivantes.
What do you need to order? _____ _____ _____ _____	De quoi avez-vous besoin pour commander ? _____ _____ _____
What do you need to practice to order your favorite foods? _____ _____ _____ _____	Que devez-vous apprendre pour commander vos plats préférés _____ _____ _____
What are the mealtimes? _____ _____ _____ _____	Quelles sont les heures des repas ? _____ _____ _____
What do you ask the waiter? _____ _____ _____ _____	Que demandez-vous au serveur ? _____ _____ _____
What does the waiter ask? _____ _____ _____ _____	Que demande le serveur ? _____ _____ _____
What do you answer the waiter? _____ _____ _____ _____	Que répondez-vous au serveur ? _____ _____ _____
What is your answer about the things on the menu? _____ _____ _____ _____	Quelle est votre réponse à propos de ce qui est au menu ? _____ _____ _____
What is your answer when you order a	Quelle est votre réponse lorsque vous

drink?	commandez une boisson ?
_____ _____ _____ _____	_____ _____ _____ _____
What are the most popular drinks? _____ _____ _____ _____	Quelles sont les boissons les plus populaires ? _____ _____ _____ _____
What phrase do you use to get the check? _____ _____ _____ _____	Quelle expression utilisez-vous pour obtenir la facture ? _____ _____ _____

Suggested answers	Réponses suggérées
What do you need to order? You need some important phrases to order.	De quoi avez-vous besoin pour commander? Vous avez besoin de quelques expressions importantes pour commander.
What do you need to practice to order your favorite foods? You need to practice some basic phrases to order your favorite foods.	Que devez-vous apprendre pour commander vos plats préférés ? Vous devez apprendre quelques expressions de base pour commander vos plats préférés.
What are the mealtimes? Breakfast, lunch and dinner are the mealtimes.	Quels sont les heures des repas ? Le petit-déjeuner, le déjeuner et le dîner sont les heures de repas.
What do you ask the waiter? The menu please.	Que demandez-vous au serveur ? Le menu, s'il vous plaît.
What does the waiter ask? Do you wish to order?	Que demande le serveur ? Souhaitez-vous passer une commande?
What do you answer the waiter? I need a minute please.	Que répondez-vous au serveur ? Donnez-moi une minute, s'il vous plaît.
What is your answer about the things on the menu? I wish to order _____.	Quelle est votre réponse à propos de ce qui est au menu ? Je souhaite commander _____.
What is your answer when you order a drink? I wish to drink _____.	Quelle est votre réponse lorsque vous commandez une boisson ? Je désire boire _____.
What are the most popular drinks? Sodas, natural juices, mineral water, coffee and tea are the most popular drinks.	Quelles sont les boissons les plus populaires? Le soda, les jus naturels, l'eau minérale, le café et le thé sont les boissons les plus populaires.
What phrase do you use to get the check? The check please.	Quelle phrase utilisez-vous pour obtenir la facture? L'addition, s'il vous plaît.

Lesson 6:
Present Simple with " ER" verbs

English How to Lose Weight	French Comment Perdre du Poids
Important vocabulary:	**Vocabulaire important :**
Running	Courir
Dancing	Danser
Decide	Décider
Diseases	Les Maladies
Eating habits	Les habitudes alimentaires
Hypertension	Hypertension
Maintain	Maintenir
Goals	Les Objectifs
Chances	Les Chances
returning	Retrouver

Every year, thousands of people **decide** to lose weight. Of course, losing weight is not an easy task, but it is not impossible. Losing weight depends on two very important factors: exercising and eating healthy. If you do these two things, your **chances** of losing weight are high.

The first factor, exercise, is the starting point. When you exercise regularly, your body stays active all the time. If you remain active, you have a high probability of **returning** to your ideal weight and size.

The ideal exercises to lose weight are aerobic. Examples of aerobic exercises are **running**, swimming, or **dancing**. Every exercise that makes you move is an ideal to way to get good results for your efforts.

The second fundamental factor for losing pounds is a healthy and balanced diet. Eating fruits and vegetables is ideal for your **goals**. You can maintain an ideal diet through simple changes to your **eating habits**. You should not eat a lot of junk food. These have many calories and little nutrition. Likewise, drinking many soft drinks and sugary drinks is not healthy. If you drink a lot of sugar, you do not lose weight. On the contrary, you gain more and more weight.

Chaque année, des milliers de personnes **décident** de perdre du poids. Bien évidemment, perdre du poids n'est pas une tâche facile, mais ce n'est pas impossible. La perte de poids dépend de deux facteurs très importants : le sport et une alimentation saine. Si vous faites ces deux choses, vos **chances** de perdre du poids sont élevées.

Le premier facteur, le sport, est le point de départ. Lorsque vous faites régulièrement des exercices, votre corps reste actif tout le temps. Si vous restez actif, vous avez de fortes chances de **retrouver** votre poids et votre taille idéale.

Les exercices idéaux pour perdre du poids sont aérobiques. Des exemples d'exercices aérobiques sont la **course**, la **natation** ou la **danse**. Chaque exercice qui vous fait bouger est un moyen idéal d'obtenir de bons résultats pour vos efforts.

Le deuxième facteur essentiel pour perdre du poids est une alimentation saine et équilibrée. Manger des fruits et des légumes est idéal pour atteindre vos **objectifs**. Vous pouvez maintenir un régime alimentaire idéal en modifiant simplement vos **habitudes alimentaires**. Vous ne devez pas manger des aliments malsains. Ceux-ci contiennent beaucoup de calories et peu de nutrition. De même, boire beaucoup de boissons gazeuses et de boissons sucrées n'est pas sain. Si vous buvez beaucoup de sucre, vous ne perdez pas de poids. Au contraire, vous prenez de plus en plus de poids.

The combination of a good diet and regular exercise is the best way to **maintain** a healthy life. The most important thing is to eat well, drink plenty of fresh water and exercise moderately three times a week. If you do this, you are on the path to a long and healthy life.

On the contrary, if you do not do this, you are in danger of **diseases** like diabetes, **hypertension** and high cholesterol. That's why you should not eat just junk food. If you eat a hamburger over the weekend, that's fine. But if you only eat this and do not eat fruits and vegetables, you are in danger of many diseases.

La combinaison d'une bonne alimentation et d'une activité physique régulière est la meilleure façon de **maintenir** une vie saine. Le plus important est de bien manger, de boire beaucoup d'eau fraîche et de faire de l'exercice trois fois par semaine de façon modérée. Si vous faites cela, vous êtes sur la voie d'une vie longue et saine.

Au contraire, si vous ne le faites pas, vous risquez de contracter des **maladies** comme le diabète, **l'hypertension** et un taux élevé de cholestérol. C'est pourquoi vous ne devrez pas seulement manger de la malbouffe. Si vous mangez un hamburger pendant le week-end, c'est très bien. Mais si vous ne mangez que cela et ne mangez pas de fruits et légumes, vous êtes exposé à de nombreuses maladies.

Please answer the following questions.	Veuillez répondre aux questions suivantes.
How many people decide to lose weight each year? _____ _____ _____ _____	Combien de personnes décident de perdre du poids chaque année? _____ _____ _____ _____
What are the two factors for losing weight? _____ _____ _____	Quels sont les deux facteurs pour perdre du poids ? _____ _____ _____
What happens when you exercise regularly? _____ _____ _____	Que se passe-t-il lorsque vous faites une activité physique régulière ? _____ _____ _____
What happens if you stay active? _____ _____ _____ _____	Que se passe-t-il lorsque vous restez actif ? _____ _____ _____
What are the ideal exercises for losing weight? _____ _____ _____ _____	Quel est le deuxième facteur pour perdre du poids ? _____ _____ _____
What is the second factor for losing weight? _____ _____ _____	Qu'est-ce que vous ne devez pas manger ? _____ _____ _____
What mustn't you eat? _____ _____ _____	Qu'est-ce que vous ne devez pas manger ? _____ _____ _____

What is the combination for maintain a healthy life? _____ _____ _____ _____	Quelle est la combinaison pour maintenir une vie saine ? _____ _____ _____ _____
If you don't have a healthy, what the diseases you get? _____ _____ _____	Si vous n'avez pas une alimentation saine, quelles sont les maladies que vous contractez? _____ _____ _____
What happens if you only eat junk food? _____ _____ _____	Que se passe-t-il si vous ne mangez que des aliments malsains ? _____ _____ _____

Suggested answers	Réponses suggérées
How many people decide to lose weight each year? Thousands of people decide to lose with every year.	Combien de personnes décident de perdre du poids chaque année ? Des milliers de personnes décident de perdre du poids chaque année.
What are the two factors for losing weight? Doing exercise and eating healthy are the two factors for losing weight.	Quels sont les deux facteurs pour perdre du poids ? Faire de l'exercice et manger sainement sont les deux facteurs pour perdre du poids.
What happens when you exercise regularly? Your body stays active when you exercise regularly.	Que se passe-t-il lorsque vous faites de l'exercice régulièrement? Votre corps reste actif lorsque vous faites de l'exercice régulièrement.
What happens if you stay active? You have a high chance of returning to your ideal weight and size.	Que se passe-t-il si vous restez actif ? Vous avez de grandes chances de retrouver votre poids et votre taille idéale.
What are the ideal exercises for losing weight? Aerobic exercises like running, swimming and dancing are ideal for losing weight.	
What is the second factor for losing weight? A balanced diet is the second factor to losing weight.	
What mustn't you eat? You mustn't eat junk food.	
What is the combination for maintain a healthy life? A balanced diet and regular exercise is the combination to maintaining a healthy life.	
If you don't have a healthy, what the diseases you get? Diabetes, hypertension and high cholesterol.	
What happens if you only eat junk food? You are in danger of many diseases.	

Section 4:
The Present Continuous Tense

Lesson 7:
Present Continuous Tense

English New Job	French Nouvel Emploi
Important vocabulary: balance sheets email graphic designer great sales manager advertising human resources secretary nice job applications	**Vocabulaire important:** Des bilans financiers Un courriel Un concepteur graphique formidable Un directeur commercial publicitaire Des ressources humaines Le/La secrétaire Agréable Des demandes d'emploi
Hi, I'm Olivia. I am 29 years old and I am a **graphic designer**. I'm happy because today is my first day at my new job. This new company is **great**. I am working as a designer for the **advertising** department. I think this is a good growth opportunity for my career.	Salut, je suis Olivia. J'ai 29 ans et je suis **graphiste**. Je suis heureuse parce qu'aujourd'hui, c'est mon premier jour dans mon nouveau travail. Cette nouvelle entreprise est **formidable**. Je travaille comme conceptrice pour le département **publicitaire**. Je pense que c'est une bonne opportunité de croissance pour ma carrière.
At this moment, I am waiting for the **human resources** manager. She is reviewing my contract. What a thrill! My contract is almost ready. The manager is only making sure that the contract has no errors. I'm so happy.	En ce moment, j'attends le directeur des **ressources humaines**. Elle est en train de revoir mon contrat. Quelle excitation ! Mon contrat est presque prêt. Le gestionnaire s'assure seulement que le contrat ne comporte aucune erreur. Je suis si heureuse.
I am thinking of so many things at this time. I am getting to know my new colleagues little by little. For example, Linda is the **secretary** of the company president. She is supporting the president in a meeting at this time.	Je pense actuellement à tant de choses. J'apprends à connaître mes nouveaux collègues au fur et à mesure. Par exemple, Linda est **secrétaire** du Directeur Général de l'entreprise. Elle accompagne le Directeur Général dans une réunion en ce moment.
Then, Veronica is the accountant of the company. She cannot talk now because she is reviewing the company's **balance sheets**. She is always doing some work task. She does not have much time to socialize, but she is very kind and	Ensuite, Veronica est la comptable de l'entreprise. Elle ne peut pas parler maintenant parce qu'elle est en train d'examiner les **états financiers**

helpful.

Juan is the **sales manager**. He is always talking on the phone. At this moment he is talking to a client. Surely, he is closing a new deal for the company. He is very **nice** and funny. I think he is a very active person.

Margarita is the assistant of the human resources manager. She is writing an **email** at this time. In the human resources department, they are always receiving **job applications**. There aren't always vacancies, but they are always looking for talented people. In short, I am super excited about this new adventure. I'm sure everyone is happy to have me on their team. I want to do my best in my new position.

And you, if you're looking for a new job, I encourage you to do your best. You sure have a lot of talent.

de l'entreprise. Elle est toujours en train de faire quelque chose. Elle n'a pas beaucoup de temps pour socialiser, mais elle est très gentille et serviable.

Juan est le **directeur de vente**. Il est toujours au téléphone. En ce moment, il parle à un client. Il est certain qu'il conclut une nouvelle affaire pour l'entreprise. Il est très **gentil** et drôle. Je pense qu'il est très dynamique.

Margarita est l'assistante du directeur des ressources humaines. Elle est en train d'écrire un **courriel**. Dans le département des ressources humaines, ils reçoivent toujours des **demandes d'emploi**. Il n'y a pas toujours des postes vacants, mais ils sont toujours à la recherche de personnes talentueuses. Bref, je suis super excitée par cette nouvelle aventure. Je suis sûr que tout le monde est heureux de m'avoir dans son équipe. Je veux donner le meilleur dans mon nouveau poste. Et vous, si vous cherchez un nouvel emploi, je vous encourage donner le meilleur de vous. Vous avez beaucoup de talent.

Please answer the following questions.	Veuillez répondre aux questions suivantes :
Why am I so happy?	Pourquoi suis-je si heureuse ?
Why is this a good opportunity?	Pourquoi est-ce une bonne occasion ?
Who am I waiting for?	Qui est-ce que j'attends ?
What is the human resources manager making sure of?	De quoi le responsable des ressources humaines s'assure-t-il ?
Whom am I getting to know?	Qui est-ce que j'apprends à connaître ?
Why can't Veronica speak now?	Pourquoi Veronica ne peut pas parler maintenant ?
Who is the sales manager?	Qui est le directeur des ventes ?
What is Margarita doing?	Que fait Margarita ?

Suggested answers	Réponses suggérées
Why am I so happy? I am happy because it is my first day at my new job.	Pourquoi suis-je si heureuse ? Je suis heureuse parce que c'est mon premier jour dans mon nouvel emploi.
Why is this a good opportunity? It is a good growth opportunity for my career.	Pourquoi est-ce une bonne occasion ? C'est une bonne opportunité de croissance pour ma carrière.
Who am I waiting for? I am waiting for the human resources manager.	Qui est-ce que j'attends ? J'attends le directeur des ressources humaines.
What is the human resources manager making sure of? She is making sure my contract has no mistakes.	De quoi le responsable des ressources humaines s'assure-t-elle ? Elle s'assure que mon contrat ne comporte aucune erreur.
Whom am I getting to know? I am getting to know my new colleagues.	Qui est-ce que j'apprends à connaître ? J'apprends à connaître mes nouveaux collègues.
Why can't Veronica speak now? She can't speak now because she is checking the company's balance sheet.	Pourquoi Veronica ne peut pas parler maintenant ? Elle ne peut pas parler maintenant parce qu'elle vérifie les états financiers de l'entreprise.
Who is the sales manager? Juan is the sales manager.	Qui est le directeur des ventes ? Juan est le directeur des ventes.
What is Margarita doing? She is writing an email at this moment.	Que fait Margarita ? Elle est en train d'écrire un courriel en ce moment.

Section 5:
The Present Simple: Irregular Verbs

Lesson 8:
Present Simple Tense: Irregular Verbs

English My Favorite Movies	Mes Films Préférés
Important vocabulary: science fiction comfort definitely documentaries educational hungry comedy series soap opera	**Vocabulaire important :** La science-fiction Le confort assurément Des documentaire éducatif Un affamé Une série comiqu Une série télévisée
We all watch movies and television series. Some people watch horror, action and romance movies. Other people watch **science fiction** movies. For me, I watch documentaries. I like interesting and **educational** films very much. I think documentaries are very important for learning new things.	Nous regardons tous des films et des séries télévisées. Certaines personnes regardent des films d'horreur, d'action et d'amour. D'autres personnes regardent des films de **science-fiction**. Moi je regarde des documentaires. J'aime beaucoup les films intéressants et **éducatifs**. Je pense que les documentaires sont très importants pour apprendre de nouvelles choses.
My sister loves television series. She sees **comedy series**. She has a lot of fun with comedies. But he also likes soap operas. She does not miss her favorite **soap opera**. This is broadcast from Monday to Friday. That is, Monday, Tuesday, Wednesday, Thursday and Friday. But, it does not air on Saturdays and Sundays. On weekends we usually go to the movies. There is always a new movie to watch. We see the premieres. Our parents also go to the movies. They watch action movies. They do not like horror movies. My parents see the highest grossing films of the moment. My sister always tells me, • You do not watch exciting	Ma sœur adore les séries télévisées. Elle voit des **séries comiques**. Elle s'amuse beaucoup avec les comédies. Mais, aime aussi les feuilletons. Elle ne manque pas son **feuilleton** préféré. Cette émission est diffusée du lundi au vendredi. C'est-à-dire lundi, mardi, mercredi, jeudi et vendredi. Mais il n'est pas diffusé les samedis et dimanches. Le week-end, on va au cinéma. Il y a toujours un nouveau film à regarder. Nous voyons les premières. Nos parents vont aussi au cinéma. Ils regardent des films d'action. Ils n'aiment pas les films d'horreur. Mes parents voient les meilleurs films du moment. Ma sœur me dit toujours,

movies. You only watch documentaries

But that's not true. We always watch interesting films in the cinema. The problem is that my sister sees a lot of horror movies. I like horror movies, but I prefer to watch documentaries. So, I learn something new. The documentaries are definitely the best.

My friends watch action movies. The movies that most enjoy are superheroes movies. Now there is a new movie of superheroes in the cinema. It is very good. But in the same way, I always watch documentaries.

What documentaries do I see?

That is a good question. I see documentaries about exotic animals, travel and history. I love travel documentaries. I see impressive landscapes and I know new cultures. These documentaries are an opportunity to travel around the world from the comfort of my home. At this moment, I'm watching a documentary about Asian food. I'm getting hungry!

-       Tu ne regardes pas de films fascinants. Vous ne regardez que des documentaires Mais ce n'est pas vrai. Nous regardons toujours des films intéressants au cinéma. Le problème, c'est que ma sœur voit beaucoup de films d'horreur. J'aime les films d'horreur, mais je préfère regarder des documentaires. Alors, j'apprends quelque chose de nouveau. Les documentaires sont définitivement les meilleurs.

Mes amis regardent des films d'action. Les films qui plaisent le plus sont les films de super-héros. Maintenant il y a un nouveau film de super-héros dans le cinéma. C'est très intéressant. Mais de la même manière, je regarde toujours des documentaires. Quels documentaires je vois?

C'est une bonne question. Je vois des documentaires sur les animaux exotiques, les voyages et l'histoire. J'adore les documentaires de voyage. Je vois des paysages impressionnants et je connais de nouvelles cultures. Ces documentaires sont l'occasion de voyager à travers le monde depuis mon domicile. En ce moment, je regarde un documentaire sur la cuisine asiatique. Je commence à avoir faim !

Please answer the following questions.	Veuillez répondre aux questions suivantes :
What do we all watch? ——————————— ——————————— ——————————— ———————————	Qu'est-ce qu'on regarde tous ? ——————————— ——————————— ——————————— ———————————
What movies do some people watch? ——————————— ——————————— ——————————— ———————————	Quels films certaines personnes regardent-elles ? ——————————— ——————————— ——————————— ———————————
What does my sister love? ——————————— ——————————— ——————————— ———————————	Qu'est-ce que ma sœur aime ? ——————————— ——————————— ——————————— ———————————
What do we do on weekends? ——————————— ——————————— ——————————— ———————————	Qu'est-ce qu'on fait le week-end ? ——————————— ——————————— ——————————— ———————————
What movies do our parents like? ——————————— ——————————— ——————————— ———————————	Quels sont les films que nos parents aiment ? ——————————— ——————————— ——————————— ———————————
What movies do I prefer to watch? ——————————— ——————————— ——————————— ———————————	Quels sont les films que je préfère regarder ? ——————————— ——————————— ——————————— ———————————
What movies do my friends like? ——————————— ——————————— ——————————— ———————————	Quels sont les films que mes amis aiment? ——————————— ——————————— ———————————
What documentaries do I watch? ——————————— ———————————	Quels documentaires dois-je regarder? ——————————— ———————————

Suggested answers	Réponses suggérées
What do we all watch? We all watch movies and TV series.	Qu'est-ce qu'on regarde tous ? Nous regardons tous des films et des séries TV.
What movies do some people watch? Some people watch terror, action and romance movies.	Quels films certaines personnes regardent-elles? Certaines personnes regardent des films d'horreur, d'action et d'amour.
What does my sister love? My sister loves to watch TV series.	Qu'est-ce que ma sœur aime? Ma sœur adore regarder les séries télévisées.
What do we do on weekends? We usually go to the movies on the weekend.	Qu'est-ce qu'on fait le week-end? D'habitude, on va au cinéma le week-end.
What movies do our parents like? Our parents like to watch the current highest-grossing movies.	Quels sont les films que nos parents aiment? Nos parents aiment regarder les meilleurs films du moment.
What movies do I prefer to watch? I prefer to watch documentaries.	Quels sont les films que je préfère regarder? Je préfère regarder des documentaires.
What movies do my friends like? My friends love to watch superhero movies.	Quels sont les films que mes amis aiment? Mes amis adorent regarder des films de super-héros.
What documentaries do I watch? I watch documentaries about exotic animals, travel and history.	Quels documentaires dois-je regarder ? Je regarde des documentaires sur les animaux exotiques, les voyages et l'histoire.

Lesson 9:
Present Simple Tense: Irregular Verbs

English What's in my Home?	French Qu'y a-t-il dans ma Maison?
Important vocabulary: bed collect intergalactic toys lamp bedside table microwave fashion fridge clothes homework suits shoes	**Vocabulaire important :** Le lit accumuler intergalactique Des jouets La lampe La table de chevet Des micro-ondes mode Le frigo Des vêtements Des devoirs Des costumes Des chaussures

• What do you have at home?

Interesting question. I have many things at home. I have all the things that serve me on a daily basis. For example, I have a **bed**, a closet, a **bedside table** and a **lamp** in my room. Also, I have my **clothes** and my **shoes**. I do not have a lot of clothes or shoes, but I have everything I need.

My parents have a very large closet in their room. My mother has a lot of clothes and shoes. He also has many jewelry and sunglasses. She always has some new clothing. He likes to keep up with **fashion**.

On the contrary, my father does not have much clothes or shoes. He has the suits he uses for work every day. He has jeans and a polo shirt, but he does not have much more than that. Actually, she has little clothes compared to my mother.

My brothers do not have a lot of clothes or shoes. But they do have many toys.

- Qu'est-ce que tu as à la maison ?

Question intéressante. J'ai beaucoup de choses à la maison. J'ai tout ce qui me sert au quotidien. Par exemple, j'ai un **lit**, un placard, une **table de chevet** et une **lampe** dans ma chambre. J'ai aussi mes **vêtements** et mes **chaussures**. Je n'ai pas beaucoup de vêtements ou de chaussures, mais j'ai tout ce dont j'ai besoin.

Mes parents ont un très grand placard dans leur chambre. Ma mère a beaucoup de vêtements et de chaussures. Elle a également de nombreux bijoux et lunettes de soleil. Elle a toujours de nouveaux vêtements. Elle aime suivre la **mode**.

Au contraire, mon père n'a pas beaucoup de vêtements ou de chaussures. Il a les costumes qu'il utilise tous les jours pour son travail. Il a un jean et un polo, mais pas plus que ça. En fait, il a peu de vêtements par rapport à ma mère. Mes frères n'ont pas beaucoup de vêtements ou de chaussures. Mais ils ont beaucoup de jouets. Ils

They collect all kinds of **toys**. Well, it's that they are still children. My brother Jorge is eight years old. My little brother, Ricardo, is six years old. They **collect** superhero toys. They play epic battles every day. When they return from school, they start **intergalactic** battles. They have a lot of fun!

We have more things in the rest of the house. In the kitchen we have the stove, the **refrigerator** and the **microwave**. We also have a large sink ... to wash the dishes ... we do not have a dishwasher. That's why I must wash the dishes.

In the family room, we have a huge television. My brothers have their video games connected to this television. But they can only play after homework. Before they cannot play. My father watches his football matches and my mother watches soap operas.

• If you have school assignments, you cannot watch television
I think I must finish my **homework** ...

collectionnent toutes sortes de **jouets**. Eh bien, c'est parce que ce sont encore des enfants. Mon frère Jorge a huit ans. Mon petit frère, Ricardo, a six ans. Ils **collectionnent** les jouets de super-héros. Ils jouent des batailles épiques tous les jours. À leur retour de l'école, ils commencent des batailles **intergalactiques**. Ils s'amusent beaucoup !

Nous avons plus de choses dans le reste de la maison. Dans la cuisine, nous avons la cuisinière, le **frigo** et la **micro-onde**. Nous avons aussi un grand évier... pour faire la vaisselle... nous n'avons pas de lave-vaisselle. C'est pourquoi je dois faire la vaisselle.

Dans la salle familiale, nous avons une énorme télévision. Mes frères ont leurs jeux vidéo connectés à cette télévision. Mais ils ne peuvent jouer qu'après les devoirs. Avant qu'ils ne puissent pas jouer. Mon père regarde ses matchs de football et ma mère regarde des feuilletons.

- Si tu as des devoirs à faire, tu ne peux pas regarder la télévision. Je pense que je dois finir mes devoirs...

Please answer the following questions.	Veuillez répondre aux questions suivantes:
What do I have at home?	Qu'est-ce que j'ai à la maison?
What do I have in my room?	Qu'est-ce que j'ai dans ma chambre?
What do my parents have in their room?	Qu'ont mes parents dans leur chambre?
What does my mother have?	Qu'est-ce que ma mère a ?
What does my father have?	Qu'est-ce que mon père a ?
What do my brothers collect?	Qu'est-ce que mes frères collectionnent ?
What do my brothers do when they come home from school?	Que font mes frères quand ils rentrent de l'école ?
What do we have in the kitchen?	Qu'avons-nous dans la cuisine ?

Suggested answers	Réponses suggérées
What do I have at home? The things that I use daily.	Qu'est-ce que j'ai à la maison ? Les choses que j'utilise quotidiennement.
What do I have in my room? I have my clothes and shoes.	Qu'est-ce que j'ai dans ma chambre ? J'ai mes vêtements et mes chaussures.
What do my parents have in their room? They have a big closet.	Qu'ont mes parents dans leur chambre? Ils ont un grand placard.
What does my mother have? My mother has a lot of clothes and shoes.	Qu'est-ce que ma mère a? Ma mère a beaucoup de vêtements et de chaussures.
What does my father have? My father has the suits he uses for work.	Qu'est-ce que mon père a ? Mon père a les costumes qu'il utilise pour le travail.
What do my brothers collect? My brothers collect all kinds of toys.	Qu'est-ce que mes frères collectionnent ? Mes frères collectionnent toutes sortes de jouets.
What do my brothers do when they come home from school? My brothers begin intergalactic battles when they come home from school.	Que font mes frères quand ils rentrent de l'école ? Mes frères commencent des batailles intergalactiques quand ils rentrent de l'école.
What do we have in the kitchen? We have a fridge and a microwave.	Qu'avons-nous dans la cuisine ? Nous avons un frigo et une micro-ondes.

Lesson 10:
Present Simple Tense: Irregular Verbs

English Careful with What You Say	French Attention à Ce Que Vous Dites
Important vocabulary: keep quiet harm deceive avoid honesty hurt bad word lie hide however truth	**Vocabulaire important :** se taire nuire abuser fuir honnêteté faire mal à vilain mot Le mensonge cacher quoi qu'il en soit La vérité
You must be careful what you say. Why?	Vous devez faire attention à ce que vous dites. Pourquoi ?
If you say something wrong, you can **hurt** a person. If you say a **bad word**, you can offend a person. If you do not tell the **truth**, you can cause some problems. This is why it is important to take care of what you say. If you tell the truth, you can avoid many problems. I always tell the truth ... well, not always. I do not like to **lie**. But being honest is always better than lying. There are times when I prefer to **keep quiet** and not tell the truth because I can hurt the feelings of others. **Honesty** is always a good quality in a person.	Si vous dites quelque chose de mal, vous pouvez **blesser** quelqu'un. Si vous dites un **mauvaismot**, vous pouvez offenser quelqu'un. Si vous ne dites pas la **vérité**, vous pouvez causer des problèmes. C'est pourquoi il est important de faire attention à ce que vous dites. Si vous dites la vérité, vous pouvez éviter de nombreux problèmes. Est-ce que je dis toujours la vérité... eh bien, pas toujours. Je n'aime pas **mentir**. Mais être honnête est toujours mieux que mentir. Il y a des moments où je préfère me **taire** et ne pas dire la vérité parce que je peux blesser les sentiments des autres. **L'honnêteté** est toujours une bonne qualité chez une personne.
However, there are many people who do not always tell the truth. Even, there are people who like to lie. It is their habit to **deceive** others. It's okay to play a joke on a person every so often. But it is not right to hide the truth. People who do not tell	**Cependant**, il y a beaucoup de gens qui ne disent pas toujours la vérité. Et même, il y a des gens qui aiment mentir. Ils ont l'habitude de **tromper** les autres. C'est normal de faire une blague à quelqu'un de

the truth do a lot of **harm** to others.

If we tell the truth all the time, we are sure that there are no deceptions. This is very important. Being honest and telling the truth are valuable attitudes in life. If you tell the truth, you are honest. Of course, there are times when it is better not to say anything. It is better to **avoid** problems.

My grandmother always says:
- If you tell the truth, people trust you because you are an honest person.

    They are very wise words. My grandmother is absolutely right. She is very wise. She always gives good advice. She always tells the truth. Sometimes she does not say anything to avoid problems. But, she is always honest with others. It does not **hide** the truth. It has no sense. It is better to tell the truth face to face.

There are times when telling the truth is not easy, but it is extremely necessary.

temps en temps. Mais il n'est pas juste de cacher la vérité. Les gens qui ne disent pas la vérité font beaucoup de **mal** aux autres. Si nous disons la vérité tout le temps, nous sommes sûrs qu'il n'y a pas de tromperies. C'est très important. Être honnête et dire la vérité sont des attitudes précieuses dans la vie. Si vous dites la vérité, vous êtes honnête. Bien sûr, il y a des moments où il vaut mieux ne rien dire. Il vaut mieux **éviter** les problèmes.

Ma grand-mère dit toujours :
-    Si tu dis la vérité, les gens te font confiance parce que tu es une personne honnête.

Ce sont des paroles très sages. Ma grand-mère a tout à fait raison. Elle est très sage. Elle donne toujours de bons conseils. Elle dit toujours la vérité. Parfois, elle ne dit rien pour éviter les problèmes. Mais, elle est toujours honnête avec les autres. Elle ne **cache** pas la vérité. Cela n'a aucun sens. Il vaut mieux dire la vérité en face. Il y a des moments où dire la vérité n'est pas facile, mais c'est extrêmement nécessaire.

Please answer the following questions.	Veuillez répondre aux questions suivantes:
What happens when you say something wrong?	Que se passe-t-il quand tu dis quelque chose de mal?
What happens if you say a bad word?	Que se passe-t-il si vous dites un mauvais mot ?
What don't I like to do?	Qu'est-ce que je n'aime pas faire ?
What is a good quality?	Qu'est-ce qu'une bonne qualité ?
What do people who like to lie do?	Que font les gens qui aiment mentir ?
What are valuable attitudes in life?	Quelles sont les attitudes importantes dans la vie ?
What does my grandmother say?	Qu'en dit ma grand-mère ?

What does my grandmother always say?	Qu'est-ce que ma grand-mère dit toujours ?
_____	_____
_____	_____
_____	_____
_____	_____

Suggested answers	Réponses suggérées
What happens when you say something wrong? You can hurt a person.	Que se passe-t-il quand tu dis quelque chose de mal ? Tu peux blesser quelqu'un.
What happens if you say a bad word? You can offend a person.	Que se passe-t-il si vous dites un mauvais mot ? Vous pouvez offenser quelqu'un.
What don't I like to do? I don't like to lie.	Qu'est-ce que je n'aime pas faire ? Je n'aime pas mentir.
What is a good quality? Honesty is always a good quality.	Qu'est-ce qu'une bonne qualité ? L'honnêteté est toujours une bonne qualité.
What do people who like to lie do? It is their custom to deceive others.	Que font les gens qui aiment mentir ? C'est leur coutume de tromper les autres.
What are valuable attitudes in life? Being honest and telling the truth are valuable attitudes.	Quelles sont les attitudes importantes dans la vie? Être honnête et dire la vérité sont des attitudes précieuses.
What does my grandmother say? If you tell the truth, other people trust you because you are an honest person.	Qu'en dit ma grand-mère? Si tu dis la vérité, les autres te font confiance parce que tu es une personne honnête.
What does my grandmother always say? My grandmother always tells the truth.	Qu'est-ce que ma grand-mère dit toujours? Ma grand-mère dit toujours la vérité.

Section 6:
Bring It All Together

Lesson 11:
Bringing it all together

English Baseball	French Le Baseball
Important vocabulary:	**Vocabulaire important :**
Acceptance	Une acceptation
accumulate	accumuler
run	courir
sport	Le sport
explanation	Une explication
out	Le dehors
less	moins
ball	Le ballon
replace	remplacer

Baseball is a **sport** played almost everywhere in the world. Maybe it's not as popular as football, but it has a lot of **acceptance** throughout the world. It is also a little understood sport in some countries of the world. Here is an **explanation** about this exciting sport.

A baseball team has nine players on the field at all times. There cannot be more nor can there be **less**. There always have to be nine players on the field. If for some reason a player is missing, the team can **replace** them with another one.

The game basically consists of the thrower, also known as the pitcher, who throws the ball to the batter. The catcher is the one who receives the ball from the pitcher. The batter must use the bat to hit the ball. If the batter hits the **ball**, but another player catches it in the air, the batter is out.

The batter has three chances to hit the ball. These opportunities are known as strike. If they **accumulate** all three strikes, they are out. But the pitcher has four chances to make three strikes. These

Le baseball est un **sport** pratiqué presque partout dans le monde. Ce n'est peut-être pas aussi populaire que le football, mais il est très bien **accepté** dans le monde entier. C'est aussi un sport peu compris dans certains pays du monde. Voici une **explication** sur ce sport passionnant.

Une équipe de baseball a neuf joueurs sur le terrain en tout temps. Il ne peut y avoir ni plus ni **moins**. Il doit toujours y avoir neuf joueurs sur le terrain. Si pour une raison quelconque un joueur manque, l'équipe peut le **remplacer** par un autre.

Le jeu consiste essentiellement en un lanceur, aussi connu sous le nom de cruche, qui relaie la balle au frappeur. Le receveur est celui qui reçoit la balle du lanceur. Le frappeur doit utiliser le bâton pour frapper la balle. Si le frappeur frappe la **balle**, mais qu'un autre joueur l'attrape dans les airs, le frappeur est retiré.

Le frappeur a trois chances de frapper la balle. Ces possibilités sont connues sous le nom de grève. S'ils **accumulent** les trois fautes, ils sont éliminés. Mais le lanceur a

opportunities are known as "balls." If the pitcher accumulates four balls, the batter must go to first base.	quatre chances de faire trois prises. Ces opportunités sont connues sous le nom de "balles". Si le lanceur accumule quatre balles, le frappeur doit se rendre au 1er but.
When the player is running around the bases, the other players can touch them with the ball to put them **out**. If the player is not running, they must stop on the base to be safe. When the player runs all the bases and arrives back to home plate, then they score a run. A run is a point in baseball. The team that scores the most runs wins.	Lorsque le joueur court autour des buts, les autres joueurs peuvent les toucher avec le ballon pour les mettre **hors-jeu**. Si le joueur ne court pas, il doit s'arrêter sur le but pour être en sécurité. Lorsque le joueur court sur tous les buts et revient au marbre, il marque un point. Une course est un point dans le baseball. L'équipe qui marque le plus de points gagne.
When a player hits the ball and it leaves the official playing field, it is known as a round tripper or home run. If there are more players running on the bases, they all score a **run**. The maximum is four runs in a home run.	Lorsqu'un joueur frappe la balle et qu'elle quitte le terrain de jeu officiel, il s'agit d'un aller-retour ou d'un "home-run". S'il y a plus de joueurs qui courent sur les buts, ils marquent tous un **point**. Le maximum est de quatre descentes dans un "home-run".

Please answer the following questions.	Veuillez répondre aux questions suivantes.
Where is baseball played?	Où joue-t-on au baseball?
How many players does a baseball team have?	Combien de joueurs compte une équipe de baseball?
What happens if a player is missing?	Que se passe-t-il si un joueur manque?
What does the game basically consist of?	En quoi consiste le jeu?
How many opportunities does the batter have?	Combien d'occasions le frappeur a-t-il?
With what does a player have to be touched in order to be out?	Avec quoi un joueur doit-il être touché pour être éliminé?

Suggested answers	Réponses suggérées
Where is baseball played? Baseball is played practically all around the world.	Où joue-t-on au baseball? Le baseball se joue pratiquement partout dans le monde.
How many players does a baseball team have? A baseball teams has nine players.	Combien de joueurs compte une équipe de baseball? Une équipe de baseball compte neuf joueurs.
What happens if a player is missing? The team can replace them with another player.	Que se passe-t-il si un joueur manque? L'équipe peut les remplacer par un autre joueur.
What does the game basically consist of? The game basically consists in the thrower, also known as the pitcher, throws the ball to the batter.	En quoi consiste le jeu? Le jeu consiste essentiellement en un lancer, aussi connu sous le nom de lanceur, qui relaie la balle au frappeur.
How many opportunities does the batter have? The batter has three opportunities to hit the ball.	Combien d'occasions le frappeur a-t-il? Le frappeur a trois occasions de frapper la balle.
With what does a player have to be touched in order to be out? The player must be touched with the ball in order to be out.	Avec quoi un joueur doit-il être touché pour être éliminé? Le joueur doit être touché avec le ballon pour être exclu.

CONCLUSION

Wow! It seems like we just got started and we are already at this point. It has certainly been an interesting trip. We hope that the contents and materials in this book have helped you to improve your overall French skills. We are certain that you have put in your best effort in order to do so.

That is why our recommendation is to go back to any of the lessons which you feel you need to review and go over the content. Of course, the more you practice, the better your skills will be. Indeed, your overall skills will improve insofar as you continue to practice.

So, do take this opportunity to continue building on your current skills. You will find that over time, you will progressively gain more and more understanding of the language you encounter on a daily basis.

Given the fact that there are a number of resources out there which can help you to practice your listening skills, such as movies, telenovelas and music, you will be able to put this content into practice right away.

Thank you once again for choosing this book. We hope to have met your expectations. And please don't forget to leave a comment. Other folks who are interested in learning French will certainly find your reviews on this book useful.

See you in the next level!